Shag

yourself slim

The most enjoyable
way to lose weight

by

Imah Goer

Crombie Jardine

PUBLISHING LIMITED
Office 2
3 Edgar Buildings
George Street
Bath
BA1 2FJ

www.crombiejardine.com

Original edition first published in paperback by
Crombie Jardine Publishing Limited in 2004
Reprinted 2004, 2005, 2006, 2007, 2009

This edition first published by
Crombie Jardine Publishing Limited in 2009

Concept and design by Alastair Williams
Written by Stewart Ferris

ISBN 978-1-906051-40-2

Printed and bound in the UK

Contents

Introduction

Losing weight isn't rocket science. Eat less and move more and it will happen. So why are so many rocket scientists obese? Simple. It's because rocket scientists are geeks and geeks don't get any sex.

The only well-shafted rocket scientists were the Nazi war criminals who built the moon rockets, but they're all long since buried with a smile on their National Socialist faces.

The link between sex and slimming is simple: a good hard rogering burns calories. If you roger hard enough then that's enough exercise to lose weight.

But do you know how much weight you'll burn up? Which positions offer the greatest slimming opportunities? Where to find a fellow slimmer willing to work with you?

No, nor did I. But that's why I researched this book. Well, that and the offer of fifty quid and a dozen free copies. Now, after literally minutes of in-depth study, you too can lose weight with a smile, just like the dead Nazis.

Each double page spread in this book features a sexual position, technique or perversion suitable for both men and women. Don't be concerned that it takes two to tango: many of the techniques can be carried out solo using accessories easily obtained from any DIY store or pie shop. From doggy style to sheep, from kissing to swinging, and from S&M to M&S, all mainstream and special interest sordid inclinations are catered for.

You can even record your calorific progress over the course of a lunar month using the handy 28 day shagging diary which has been cynically provided at almost zero cost by the publishers in order to use up space at the end of this book.

So throw away the diet books, organic brown rice and fitness DVDs (except for the ones with saucy celebs in body-hugging lycra). Your weight loss regime starts now, right inside your undies. Counting calories has never been this much fun!

Self-shagging with a porn mag

Walking to the newsagent
for a porn mag
40 calories

Carrying home lots of computer
mags to hide the porn mag
50 calories

The actual hand shandy
35 calories

☆ TOTAL: 125 calories ☆

Self-shagging with a washing machine

Loading the washing machine
and switching it on
10 calories

Sitting on it during the
fastest spin cycle
30 calories

Ironing the clothes afterwards
30 calories

☆ TOTAL: 70 calories ☆

Self-shagging with the Internet

Clicking the mouse to find
a suitable porn site
3 calories

The actual hand shandy
35 calories

Wiping clean the
computer screen
10 calories

☆ **TOTAL: 48 calories** ☆

Self-shagging with a vibrator

Replacing the batteries that short-circuited last time due to damp conditions
10 calories

Letting the machine do the work
2 calories

A far bigger orgasm than your boyfriend ever gives you
100 calories

☆ **TOTAL: 112 calories** ☆

Self-shagging with an inflatable doll

Blowing up the doll by mouth
35 calories

Repairing leaks with sticky tape
5 calories

Doing it doggy style because
the doll's face stinks from
a previous encounter
40 calories

☆ **TOTAL: 80 calories** ☆

Self-shagging with a banana

Walking to the supermarket
45 calories

Peeling, inserting and
shagging the banana
5 calories

Spending ages trying get
bits of semi-dissolved
banana out of your twat
10 calories

☆ TOTAL: 60 calories ☆

Self-shagging with a steak & kidney pie

Buying the ingredients with
a dirty grin on your face
25 calories

Making a pie with a hole
in the crust for 'ventilation'
10 calories

Giving the pie a good seeing-to
40 calories

☆ **TOTAL: 75 calories** ☆

Finding a shag partner in a club

Pretending to be able to
dance in a nightclub
70 calories

Plucking up the courage
to use a chat-up line
15 calories

Running away from
his girlfriend
85 calories

☆ TOTAL: 170 calories ☆

Finding a shag partner on holiday

Holding your stomach in whilst
walking along the beach looking
for a suitable partner
40 calories

Buying an ice-cream and
sharing it with a stranger
minus 200 calories

Holding your stomach
in even more
50 calories

☆ **TOTAL:
minus 110 calories** ☆

Finding a shag partner in the gym

Twenty minutes on the treadmill
getting ignored by everyone
300 calories

10 minutes on the bike
getting ignored by everyone
150 calories

Giving up and staggering home
50 calories

☆ **TOTAL: 500 calories** ☆

Preparing for a shag

Taking a shower or bath
even though you weren't due
to have one for another week
10 calories

Brushing your teeth *and* flossing
and using mouthwash
5 calories

Trying on kinky underwear
10 calories

☆ **TOTAL: 25 calories** ☆

Preparing for a shag

Trying on 15 different outfits,
none of which disguise
your extra pounds
20 calories

Squeezing your arse into tiny
trousers meant for a 10 year old
5 calories

Taking it all off again now
that you've seduced him
10 calories

☆ TOTAL: 35 calories ☆

Preparing for a shag

Undoing her bra with one hand
5 calories

Removing her arse from
too-tight jeans with the help
of some margarine and a
team of firemen
20 calories

Shaking hands with the
firemen as they leave
5 calories

☆ **TOTAL: 30 calories** ☆

Preparing for a shag

Starting to undo his jeans
before he's turned on
5 calories

Removing his jeans
once he gets excited
10 calories

Undressing the rest of
him with your teeth
10 calories

☆ **TOTAL: 25 calories** ☆

Safe shagging - security

Locking the bedroom door
5 calories

Constructing an alibi so
your wife doesn't find out
5 calories

Giving your shag partner a false
telephone number so she can't track
you down if you give her anything
besides pleasure
5 calories

☆ **TOTAL: 15 calories** ☆

Safe shagging
- tight condoms

Unwrapping the condom
10 calories

Struggling to put on the condom when
it's an impressively tight fit
15 calories

Hiding the used condom behind the
radiator so scientists in the future can
clone you from your spunk
5 calories

☆ TOTAL: 30 calories ☆

Safe shagging - loose condoms

Unwrapping the condom
10 calories

Slipping on a condom that's
embarrassingly loose and
blaming the room temperature
5 calories

Groping yourself repeatedly
during the performance to
try to hold the condom in place
20 calories

☆ TOTAL: 35 calories ☆

Foreplay - dancing

Dancing a strip-tease
around the room while singing
'You can leave your hat on'
60 calories

Throwing your clothes
across the bedroom floor
15 calories

Putting everything back on
again because this was just a
rehearsal and your partner
hasn't arrived yet
5 calories

☆ **TOTAL: 80 calories** ☆

Foreplay - oiling

Covering your body
with lavender oil
10 calories

Covering your woman's
body with lavender oil
20 calories

Putting a towel on the bed
so your sheets don't get
covered in lavender oil
5 calories

☆ **TOTAL: 35 calories** ☆

Foreplay - massage

Giving your man a full
length massage on his back
60 calories

Waking your man up
after the massage
sends him to sleep
5 calories

Rolling your sleepy man
over for the good bits
10 calories

☆ TOTAL: 75 calories ☆

Foreplay - groping

Groping one erogenous zone
(fully clothed)
10 calories

Groping two erogenous zones
at the same time (fully clothed)
20 calories

Groping three erogenous zones at the
same time (fully clothed)
30 calories

☆ **TOTAL: 60 calories** ☆

Foreplay - kissing

Kissing your partner's neck
5 calories

Kissing your partner's lips
5 calories

Kissing with tongues
10 calories

Wiping the saliva off your lips using
your partner's hair
5 calories

☆ TOTAL: 25 calories ☆

Foreplay - nibbling

Nibbling your partner's ears
5 calories

Nibbling your partner's fingers
5 calories

Nibbling your partner's nipples
5 calories

Nibbling your partner's
cream cakes
minus 300 calories

☆ TOTAL:
minus 285 calories ☆

Foreplay - stimulating

Countering the effects of brewer's droop in your drunk partner by using your hand
5 calories

Countering the effects of brewer's droop in your drunk partner by using your mouth
5 calories

Jumping on top of him quickly before he passes out
10 calories

☆ TOTAL: 20 calories ☆

Foreplay
- golden shower

Persuading your partner
to let you piss on her
2 calories

Pissing on your partner
5 calories

Running away from your angry
partner who thought you
were only kidding
100 calories

☆ **TOTAL: 107 calories** ☆

Foreplay - bondage

Putting on various items
of leather clothing
5 calories

Locking your partner to the bed
with a pair of furry handcuffs
5 calories

Cutting off the handcuffs with
a hacksaw after you realise
you've lost the keys
100 calories

☆ TOTAL: 110 calories ☆

Foreplay - S&M

Making your man lick
your shoes while you
spank his bare bottom
5 calories

Making your man sit in a dog
kennel while you watch telly
2 calories

Opening a tin of dog food
and making him eat out of
the dog's bowl with his face
5 calories

☆ **TOTAL: 12 calories** ☆

Foreplay - M&S

Choosing new M&S underwear
5 calories

Winking at your woman to join
you in the changing rooms
2 calories

Realising this store doesn't
have changing rooms and
being forced to have sex at
home like everyone else
5 calories

☆ TOTAL: 12 calories ☆

Foreplay
- whilst driving

Getting her tits out with
one hand on the wheel
10 calories

Having a fish and finger pie whilst
keeping an eye on the road
20 calories

Thinking of an excuse for
the accident to write on
the insurance form
5 calories

☆ **TOTAL: 35 calories** ☆

38

Foreplay
- whilst driving

Undoing his trousers with
one hand on the wheel
5 calories

When faced with two
sticks remembering which
one to use to change gear
2 calories

Realising windscreen wipers
won't clean on the inside
2 calories

☆ **TOTAL: 9 calories** ☆

Foreplay - oral

Chucking your woman
in the shower,
especially if she's French
5 calories

Giving her a good seeing-to
with your tongue
50 calories

Rinsing the pubes out
of your mouth
5 calories

☆ **TOTAL: 60 calories** ☆

Foreplay - oral

Chucking your man
in the shower,
whether or not he's French
5 calories

Licking his lollipop
until it explodes
50 calories

Bravely deciding to swallow
instead of spitting
minus 200 calories

☆ TOTAL:
minus 145 calories ☆

Foreplay - 69

Getting into position
5 calories

Stopping to explain that
she's meant to being gobbling
you while you gobble her
5 calories

Enjoying a hairy pie while
your lollipop is licked
40 calories

☆ **TOTAL: 50 calories** ☆

Foreplay - 69

Getting into position
5 calories

Enjoying yourself even
though his nob keeps
bashing you in the face
20 calories

Sucking his snake while
your bean enjoys a good
tongue flicking
40 calories

☆ TOTAL: 65 calories ☆

Shagging
- doggy style

Taking her from behind
20 calories

Moving her around a bit so
you can still see the telly
10 calories

Giving her the best session
she's had since she once got
too friendly with an Alsation
75 calories

☆ **TOTAL: 105 calories** ☆

Shagging
- doggy style

Letting him take you
from behind
10 calories

Straining your neck up so
you can see the telly too
10 calories

Wishing you still lived
next door to that Alsation
5 calories

☆ **TOTAL: 25 calories** ☆

Shagging
- missionary

Spreading her legs
5 calories

Enjoying yourself while
she pretends to
75 calories

Rolling over, farting,
and falling asleep
5 calories

☆ **TOTAL: 85 calories** ☆

Shagging
- missionary

Spreading your legs
5 calories

Faking pleasure and an
orgasm whilst thinking about
what to wear tomorrow
50 calories

Getting up and going out to
have some fun once
he's passed out
200 calories

☆ **TOTAL: 255 calories** ☆

Shagging - in the car

Climbing into the back seat
5 calories

Contorting yourself into an
uncomfortable position
ready to attempt entry
10 calories

Pulling your clothes back on quickly
when a friendly neighbour taps on the
window to see if you're OK
20 calories

☆ **TOTAL: 35 calories** ☆

Shagging
- in the car

Lying awkwardly on the back seat
5 calories

Trying to stop him squashing you
while he gets into position
20 calories

Hiding your face when the
neighbour opens the door and sees
your knickers round your ankles
5 calories

☆ **TOTAL: 30 calories** ☆

Shagging
- on the car bonnet

Helping her onto the bonnet
5 calories

Doing it to her gently in
case the bonnet gets dented
55 calories

Panicking when you see the
shape of her bum cheeks
embedded into the metal
25 calories

☆ TOTAL: 85 calories ☆

Shagging
- on the car bonnet

Enjoying the feeling of the
warm engine under your arse
5 calories

Enjoying the feeling of the
fresh night air on your twat
5 calories

Helping him to straighten out
the dent in the bonnet
100 calories

☆ TOTAL: 110 calories ☆

Shagging
- at the movies

Walking to a subtle back
row seat in the corner
5 calories

Eating a gallon of popcorn
minus 300 calories

Timing your shag noises to
the sounds in the film
30 calories

☆ **TOTAL:**
minus 265 calories ☆

Shagging
- at the movies

Lifting up your skirt
and sitting on him
5 calories

Waiting for him to finish his popcorn
2 calories

Trying to show no expression when
people turn round to see what the
noise is all about
40 calories

☆ **TOTAL: 47 calories** ☆

Shagging
- her on top

Lying on your back groping her tits
while she sits on you
10 calories

Letting her do all the work
0 calories

Making a few token thrusts so she
doesn't get bored and stop
25 calories

☆ TOTAL: 35 calories ☆

Shagging
- her on top

Climbing onto him while
he gropes your tits
15 calories

Doing all the work
150 calories

Getting bored and stopping because
he's making no effort
0 calories

☆ **TOTAL: 165 calories** ☆

Shagging
- in a porn film

Having to 'keep wood' for hours at a
time during multiple takes
300 calories

Having to shag dozens
of birds in a day's work
500 calories

Feeling guilty that you have
such a great job while your
mates work in a pie factory
10 calories

☆ TOTAL: 810 calories ☆

Shagging
- in a porn film

Allowing access to parts of you
that are normally exits only
20 calories

Trying to keep moist under
the hot studio lights
100 calories

Faking orgasm twenty
times in a day
300 calories

 **TOTAL: 420 calories** ☆

Shagging
- silently

Trying to find a sexual position
that won't make the bed creak
and wake up your housemates
40 calories

Forcing yourself to pump slowly
so that you don't grunt too much
40 calories

Muffling the sound of your orgasm
by burying your face into her tits
20 calories

☆ TOTAL: 100 calories ☆

Shagging
- silently

Lying still, not needing
to fake enjoyment
5 calories

Bracing your arms against
the wall to muffle
the bed's vibrations
60 calories

Worrying that your friends will
think you're having an epileptic fit
and storm in to save you
10 calories

☆ TOTAL: 75 calories ☆

Shagging
- noisily

Thrusting as hard as possible
with the aim of breaking the bed
200 calories

Howling with delight at
the top of your voice
10 calories

Repairing the wooden
slats under the bed
70 calories

☆ TOTAL: 280 calories ☆

FOR HER

Shagging - noisily

Rolling over every couple of
minutes to change positions
in a fervour of passion
200 calories

Thumping the mattress
in orgasmic ecstasy
30 calories

Phoning your boyfriend to tell him
you're ready to see him now
5 calories

☆ **TOTAL: 235 calories** ☆

Shagging - a prostitute

Asking various women how much they charge before finding an actual prozzie
20 calories

Explaining to her that your wife doesn't understand you
10 calories

Stopping half way through to see if you have enough cash to touch both nipples
20 calories

☆ TOTAL: 50 calories ☆

Shagging
- a client

Explaining the tariff
5 calories

Listening to his bullshit about
his wife not understanding him
5 calories

Removing his hands from
your breasts and explaining
they're optional extras
20 calories

☆ TOTAL: 30 calories ☆

Shagging
- up the arse

Persuading her you got the
wrong hole by accident
but now you're there...
10 calories

Giving her one right up there
70 calories

Washing your nob, your
duvet, your pillowcases
and sheets...twice
20 calories

☆ **TOTAL: 100 calories** ☆

Shagging
- up the arse

Recoiling in horror when you
realise what he's doing
10 calories

Letting him give you one right up there
whilst wondering whether to mention
your diarrhoea problem
40 calories

Apologising to him while he washes
everything in the room twice
5 calories

☆ **TOTAL: 55 calories** ☆

Shagging
- your teacher

Reading her your crappy
poems to seduce her
10 calories

Indulging in sexual techniques you
never dreamed were possible
250 calories

Trying to chat up your
replacement teacher after the first one
gets fired for shagging you
10 calories

☆ TOTAL: 270 calories ☆

Shagging
- your teacher

Flirting in class by pointing your
breasts provocatively at him
10 calories

Getting disillusioned by his lack of
sexual imagination in bed
50 calories

Blackmailing him to give
you good grades in return
for keeping his job
10 calories

☆ TOTAL: 70 calories ☆

Shagging
- a sheep

Seducing it by wearing your favourite
woolly jumper and talking
knowledgeably about grass
20 calories

Mounting it from behind
while it's still thinking about your
comments on lawn upkeep
50 calories

Running away from
the jealous farmer
300 calories

☆ TOTAL: 370 calories ☆

Shagging
- a sheep

Putting on several sets
of false breasts to attract
a male sheep
20 calories

Letting your chosen ruminant
mammal take you from behind
30 calories

Running away from
the excited farmer
300 calories

☆ TOTAL: 350 calories ☆

Shagging
- a nervous virgin

Spending three days giving her
foreplay and still she won't relax
500 calories

Trying to persuade her
that you're the best person
to lose her cherry to
20 calories

Giving up and heading into
the loo for a wank instead
50 calories

☆ TOTAL: 570 calories ☆

Shagging
- a nervous virgin

Wondering why you're
bothering to go to bed with
such a nerd in the first place
10 calories

Intimidating him with your sexual
confidence and experience
20 calories

Telling him it's quite normal
to ejaculate before he's
even got his pants off
10 calories

☆ TOTAL: 40 calories ☆

Shagging
- a desperate virgin

Trying to restrain her enthusiasm
before she wears out your nob
50 calories

Persuading her that all men
are as bad as you in bed
10 calories

Carving a notch in your
bedpost to record the event
30 calories

☆ TOTAL: 90 calories ☆

Shagging
- a desperate virgin

Explaining what foreplay is for whilst
holding him away from you
5 calories

Enjoying a full 30 seconds
of foreplay from him before
he gets down to it
20 calories

Enjoying a further 30 seconds
of full-blown bonking before
he explodes
40 calories

☆ **TOTAL: 65 calories** ☆

Shagging
- two birds

Almost creaming your pants
when you realise two birds are
prepared to go to bed with you
20 calories

Worrying they won't be satisfied
with you and might demand a
second bloke to help
10 calories

Working twice as hard as normal to
keep them both satisfied
330 calories

☆ TOTAL: 360 calories ☆

Shagging
- two blokes

Offering up both ends of
yourself at the same time
200 calories

Offering two modes of access to your
lower end at the same time
200 calories

Not being able to sit
down for a week
400 calories

☆ **TOTAL: 800 calories** ☆

Shagging
- with another couple

Introducing 'er indoors
to his missus
5 calories

Making polite conversation
about house prices in your area
5 calories

Giving his missus a full
10,000 mile service while he
takes a ride in the loan car
150 calories

☆ **TOTAL: 160 calories** ☆

Shagging
- with another couple

Worrying whether the men
prefer her boobs to yours
5 calories

Worrying whether your man
will feel inadequate when he sees
you enjoying a bigger cock
5 calories

Worrying whether the
other woman might really
be a tuppence licker
5 calories

☆ TOTAL: 15 calories ☆

Shagging
- orgies

Awkwardly removing your
suit, wondering if you've
turned up at the right house
10 calories

Groping more people at
once than you can count
100 calories

Realising this isn't the
wake you were invited to and
putting your clothes back on
30 calories

☆ **TOTAL: 140 calories** ☆

Shagging
- orgies

Living out your every fantasy
in the anonymity of a mass
of heaving bodies
250 calories

Realising with horror that
you forgot to take your pill today
10 calories

Narrowing the father of the baby
down to just 15 possible men
40 calories

☆ **TOTAL: 300 calories** ☆

Shagging
- with a celebrity

Working out in the gym for
three months to get fit
enough to attract a celebrity
50,000 calories

Showing your six-pack to a famous
bird at a glamorous London party
5 calories

Giving her the night of her
life by taking her back to your
bedsit for a shag and a pizza
300 calories

☆ TOTAL: 50,305 calories ☆

Shagging
- with a celebrity

Putting on a transparent top that
reveals your invisible bra and your
pneumatic knockers
5 calories

Rubbing your jugs up against an
unsuspecting TV presenter while
asking him the way to the bogs
20 calories

Selling your story to the
The Sun the next day
10 calories

☆ TOTAL: 35 calories ☆

Shagging
- like a celebrity

Building a swimming pool
in your back garden
25,000 calories

Inviting loads of birds to come
and party with you in the pool
50 calories

Giving up waiting for them to
arrive and paying for prostitutes to
provide your glamour instead
30 calories

☆ **TOTAL: 25,080 calories** ☆

Shagging
- like a celebrity

Finding a man so much
younger than you that you'd
be too embarrassed to
introduce him to your friends
70 calories

Doing it in the garden so that the
paparazzi can photograph you
100 calories

Enrolling at a clinic to
treat your sex addiction
40 calories

☆ TOTAL: 210 calories ☆

Shagging
- on Big Brother

Practising by choking
your chicken under the
duvet without making any
noise or visible movement
100 calories

Carrying out foreplay with her
in the hot tub under the bubbles
60 calories

Giving up hiding and shagging live in
front of millions of students
300 calories

☆ **TOTAL: 460 calories** ☆

Shagging
- on Big Brother

Talking endlessly about your
boyfriend back home whilst massaging
a naked fellow contestant
100 calories

Denying to the other housemates
that you two are an item
20 calories

Giving him one secretly under
the duvet while the whole world
thinks he's just having a wank
200 calories

☆ **TOTAL: 320 calories** ☆

Shagging
- swingers

Realising you're lower middle class,
middle aged and slightly ugly
10 calories

Realising your equally ugly
wife no longer turns you on
10 calories

Coupling with swingers
because it's the only way
you can get it up at your age
300 calories

☆ **TOTAL: 320 calories** ☆

Shagging
- swingers

Making much more effort to clean
and polish yourself than you ever
did for your husband
100 calories

Making sure your husband
washes his balls
20 calories

Doing it with other couples because
you still have needs but don't
fancy the hassle of divorce
300 calories

☆ **TOTAL: 420 calories** ☆

Shagging - in front of a romantic fire

Chopping the romantic wood
200 calories

Lighting the romantic firelighters
10 calories

Shagging her on a nice
rug whilst keeping an eye
on the romantic flames in
case they die down
200 calories

☆ **TOTAL: 410 calories** ☆

Shagging
- in front of a
romantic fire

Watching telly while he's
outside chopping the firewood
0 calories

Drinking a glass of plonk while he
struggles to get the damn thing lit
minus 80 calories

Being rogered on the floor whilst
worrying if the rug will catch fire
200 calories

☆ TOTAL: 120 calories ☆

Shagging
- a really fat bird

Helping her up the stairs
into your bedroom and
administering oxygen
100 calories

Heaving her up onto the
bed and hoping the
floorboards hold
100 calories

Humping her as if
you're on a bouncy castle
100 calories

☆ **TOTAL: 300 calories** ☆

Shagging
- a really fat bloke

Undoing the long rope that's
holding up his trousers
5 calories

Helping him locate his
nob somewhere under
his sagging stomach
20 calories

Insisting that it's probably
better if *you* go on top
10 calories

☆ TOTAL: 35 calories ☆

Shagging
- up against a wall

Building a wall
(best to use bricks and mortar - it's
stronger than plasterboard)
500 calories

Leaning your lady up
against it and lifting her skirt
10 calories

Entering her gently in case
the wall gives way
60 calories

☆ TOTAL: 570 calories ☆

Shagging
- up against a wall

Bracing yourself against a wall
with your knickers round one ankle
and your skirt lifted high
20 calories

Hoping someone will come
along soon to give you a good
shagging before you catch a chill
10 calories

Realising you can't put much into the
shag from that position
10 calories

☆ **TOTAL: 40 calories** ☆

Shagging
- the wheelbarrow
position

Locating your nearest garden centre
50 calories

Putting your naked woman
into a wheelbarrow
30 calories

Admitting to the security guard that
you didn't really understand what
this sex position involves
30 calories

☆ TOTAL: 110 calories ☆

94

Shagging
- the wheelbarrow
position

Getting down on all fours and pointing
your arse up at him
10 calories

Letting him lift your legs so
your weight is all on your hands
30 calories

Collapsing forwards onto your arms as
he tries to roger you from behind
10 calories

☆ TOTAL: 50 calories ☆

Shagging
- cyber sex

Positioning your webcam so that
your irresistible body can be seen
by all those men pretending
to be girls on the Internet
5 calories

Spending many hours online trying to
find a genuine bird to cyber-shag
10 calories

Making do with a Thai ladyboy
30 calories

☆ TOTAL: 45 calories ☆

Shagging
- cyber sex

Setting up your webcam
in front of your bed
5 calories

Re-setting your computer when
it turns out your naked presence
has overloaded the servers with
too many masturbating males
5 calories

Touching yourself watched by a million
lonely men with their dicks out
100 calories

☆ TOTAL: 110 calories ☆

Shagging
- side by side

Deciding you can't be bothered
to go on top and wondering whether
you can enter her from the side
5 calories

Trying to lift her chubby
thighs out of the way
20 calories

Wiggling your backside a bit
while you try to enter before giving up
and going down the pub
30 calories

☆ **TOTAL: 55 calories** ☆

Shagging
- side by side

Persuading him not to
go to the pub just yet
5 calories

Sliding close to him and
wrapping your legs around him
10 calories

Deciding it would have been
better to make the effort to
go on top in the first place
5 calories

☆ **TOTAL: 20 calories** ☆

Shagging
- spoons position

Cuddling up behind your
partner while she's asleep
5 calories

Trying to take her gently from
behind in rhythm to her snores
20 calories

Feeling insulted that
your erection wasn't enough
to disturb her sleep
5 calories

☆ TOTAL: 30 calories ☆

Shagging
- spoons position

Lying in bed quietly minding
your own business,
pretending to be asleep
5 calories

Trying not to react to feeling a small
prick between your legs
5 calories

Lying in bed gloating that he thinks his
nob is too small to wake you up
5 calories

☆ TOTAL: 15 calories ☆

Shagging
- in the shower

Getting the water
temperature right
10 calories

Soaping her up
10 calories

Trying not to slip over while
you're slipping her one
80 calories

☆ **TOTAL: 100 calories** ☆

Shagging
- in the shower

Standing on a chair so he can
enter you without slipping a disc
10 calories

Soaping him up
10 calories

Enjoying five minutes of
precarious passion
80 calories

☆ **TOTAL: 100 calories** ☆

Shagging
- mile high club

Queuing up for the bogs
at the back of the plane
10 calories

Squeezing into the tiny cubicle
with your woman while other
passengers stare suspiciously
10 calories

Shagging her on the sink so
vigorously that the pilot illuminates
the 'fasten seat belts' sign
150 calories

☆ **TOTAL: 170 calories** ☆

Shagging
- mile high club

Having a quick piss
before inviting your man into
the cubicle to join you
10 calories

Sitting on the sink with the tap poking
into your arse while he porks you
120 calories

Sheepishly walking back past
the queue of angry passengers
about to wet themselves
10 calories

☆ **TOTAL: 140 calories** ☆

Shagging
- faking orgasm

Hiding a small sachet of salad
cream in your underpants
5 calories

Screaming loudly while bursting the
salad cream packet over her
20 calories

Wishing you hadn't just spanked your
monkey before meeting her
5 calories

☆ TOTAL: 30 calories ☆

Shagging
- faking orgasm

Howling like a dog (whose tail
has just been trodden on)
10 calories

Thumping the bed
with your arms
10 calories

Forcing a contented grin
on your unsatisfied face
10 calories

☆ TOTAL: 30 calories ☆

Shagging
- real orgasm

Grunting like a pig
20 calories

Shafting her like a steam piston
engine until the boiler blows up
200 calories

Falling asleep and snoring
5 calories

☆ TOTAL: 225 calories ☆

Shagging
- real orgasm

Getting a warm feeling
around your backside
10 calories

Feeling electricity running through
every nerve in your body
40 calories

Realising you've ripped
open the old electric blanket
10 calories

☆ TOTAL: 60 calories ☆

Shagging
- telephone sex

Dialling a pervy line from the
back of the *Sunday Sport*
5 calories

Tapping your foot impatiently while a
recorded voice reminds you that the
cost of this call will bankrupt you
5 calories

Jerking off to the voice of a rancid
warty former whore
50 calories

☆ **TOTAL: 60 calories** ☆

Shagging
- telephone sex

Dialling a dodgy sex line number
because your girlfriends dared you to
5 calories

Finding the voice on the other end
surprisingly dishy and wishing you
could flick your bean
10 calories

Flicking your bean anyway and
hoping they won't notice
40 calories

☆ **TOTAL: 55 calories** ☆

Extra calorific benefits of shagging

Looking for the
condom afterwards
20 calories

Being forced to change
the bedsheets before your
wife comes home
50 calories

Walking to the clap clinic
40 calories

☆ **TOTAL: 110 calories** ☆

Extra calorific benefits of shagging

Losing your appetite at
the mere thought of him
seeing your love handles
200 calories

Being shagged so hard it
takes an extra effort just to
walk for the next two days
100 calories

Walking to your friend's house to tell
her about your sordid night
40 calories

☆ **TOTAL: 340 calories** ☆

Negative calorific aspects of shagging

Drinking 5 pints of lager to
pluck up the courage to
ask her out in the first place
minus 300 calories

Licking chocolate and
cream off her boobs
minus 400 calories

Having a big fry-up the next
morning when you sober up
minus 500 calories

☆ **TOTAL:**
minus 1200 calories ☆

Negative calorific aspects of shagging

Being seduced with rich food
and lots of alcohol
minus 600 calories

Swallowing instead of spitting
minus 150 calories

Getting the munchies after
a good hard rogering
minus 300 calories

☆ **TOTAL:**
minus 1050 calories ☆

Shagging diary

day 1

Sex positions attempted	Calories burned

TOTAL CALORIES:

Shagging diary
day 2

Sex positions attempted

Calories burned

TOTAL CALORIES:

Shagging diary
day 3

Sex positions attempted

Calories burned

TOTAL CALORIES:

118

Shagging diary
day 4

Sex positions attempted

Calories burned

TOTAL CALORIES:

Shagging diary
day 5

Sex positions attempted

Calories burned

TOTAL CALORIES:

Shagging diary

day 6

Sex positions attempted

Calories burned

TOTAL CALORIES:

Shagging diary

day 7

Sex positions attempted	Calories burned

TOTAL CALORIES:

Shagging diary
day 8

Sex positions attempted

Calories burned

TOTAL CALORIES:

Shagging diary
day 9

Sex positions attempted

Calories burned

TOTAL CALORIES:

Shagging diary
day 10

Sex positions attempted

Calories burned

TOTAL CALORIES:

Shagging diary
day 11

Sex positions attempted	Calories burned

TOTAL CALORIES:

Shagging diary
day 12

Sex positions attempted

Calories burned

TOTAL CALORIES:

Shagging diary
day 13

Sex positions attempted	Calories burned

TOTAL CALORIES:

Shagging diary
day 14

Sex positions attempted

Calories burned

TOTAL CALORIES:

Shagging diary
day 15

Sex positions attempted

Calories burned

TOTAL CALORIES:

Shagging diary
day 16

Sex positions attempted

Calories burned

TOTAL CALORIES:

Shagging diary
day 17

Sex positions attempted

Calories burned

TOTAL CALORIES:

Shagging diary
day 18

Sex positions attempted | **Calories burned**

TOTAL CALORIES:

Shagging diary

day 19

Sex positions attempted	Calories burned

TOTAL CALORIES:

Shagging diary
day 20

Sex positions attempted

Calories burned

TOTAL CALORIES:

Shagging diary
day 21

Sex positions attempted	Calories burned

TOTAL CALORIES:

Shagging diary
day 22

Sex positions attempted

Calories burned

TOTAL CALORIES:

Shagging diary
day 23

Sex positions attempted	Calories burned

TOTAL CALORIES:

Shagging diary
day 24

**Sex positions
attempted**

**Calories
burned**

TOTAL CALORIES:

Shagging diary
day 25

Sex positions attempted	Calories burned
TOTAL CALORIES:	

Shagging diary
day 26

Sex positions attempted	Calories burned

TOTAL CALORIES:

Shagging diary

day 27

Sex positions attempted

Calories burned

TOTAL CALORIES:

Shagging diary
day 28

Sex positions attempted

Calories burned

TOTAL CALORIES:

www.crombiejardine.com